Find your
CALLING

DISCOVERING WHAT YOU'RE MEANT TO DO: A 21-DAY GUIDE FOR HIM

BY DALE PARTRIDGE

StartupCamp.com a DBA of Dale Partridge, Inc.
70 S.W. Century Drive. #100-503
Bend, Oregon 97702
www.StartupCamp.com

Ordering Information:
Quantity sales. Special discounts are available on quantity purchases by corporations, associations, and others. For details, contact the publisher at the address above or by email at support@startupcamp.com

Printed in the United States of America

Category: Self-Help
Partridge, Dale.
Find Your Calling : Discovering What You're Meant To Do: A 21-Day Guide For Him / Dale Partridge

ISBN-13: 978-0692801703

First Edition

TABLE OF CONTENTS

00: MY STORY

Several years ago I was devastated when a friend I admired leaned across the dinner table and called me the B-word. No, not that one. He called me "busy."

"You do a lot of stuff, Dale. You always have new projects and new ideas," he said. "But you seem scattered... almost like you don't know what you're meant to do. So, I'm just going to ask you, do you?"

His bold question caught me off-guard and I froze.

I fumbled my way through the rest of our conversation, defending myself and my schedule. I threw out convoluted reasons for my muddled mess of a pursuit. I left the dinner table that night embarrassed and convicted about not having a clear answer to his question.

In that moment, though, I decided to put to death my aimless aspirations and abandon the purposeless life where many find themselves trapped. Ultimately, my friend's query sent me on a journey to discover my calling, and that journey has been one of the most rewarding of my life.

What about you? Are you a man living the 'reactive' life—never making steps toward an identified destination? Do you just respond to whatever is presented to you?

Most men I know—particularly entrepreneurs and business leaders—judge their lives by their calendars. They have unlimited tasks dotting their to-do lists and mountains of emails piled in their inboxes. Their calendars are full, their lives are full, and they have no idea where they're going.

Your calling is a mountaintop destination that can only be discovered by you. It's found as you develop your natural gifts and it culminates in the realization of your life's greatest work. It's a journey that allows men to feel vibrant, meaningful, and important.

I believe every man, including you, has a unique

calling—though most haven't found theirs. While it's not impossible to identify, it can be difficult to discover. We have to work to find and unleash it.

I wish I could tell you that after my friend confronted me about my distracted pursuits, I discovered my calling the next day and my life has been sensational ever since. But the conversation only launched a frustrating journey in which I explored a variety of different routes leading only to dead-end streets and quick-turn cul-de-sacs. Along the way I discovered a series of principles and practices that clarified my calling and can help you discover yours.

This book is a field guide to help men move from a busy life to a called one. While the information is arranged in 21 chronological days, you don't have to complete the journey in three quick weeks. Take your time and don't be afraid to return to one of the day's entries if you need to spend more time with it. This process shouldn't be hurried. Purpose to stay focused so that you don't miss, misread, or confuse what you're learning about your unique calling.

Although this book is short, it isn't easy. I'm asking you to make uncomfortable choices and difficult decisions. If you're looking for a quick painless process to live a life of meaning, this book is not for you. This book demands maturity. It insists on your understanding the difference between 'should' and 'could,' 'smart' and 'right.' I'll challenge you not to allow what you want to do to prevent what you're meant to do.

Furthermore, this book unfolds progressively. Like the movement toward your calling, it gets better as you get further into it! The lessons dive deeper, the activities reveal more, and the implications become evident. Avoid speed-reading or shortcuts. Trust the map and trust the guide.

Believe me when I say this, gentlemen: living without a clear sense of calling is a prison sentence. But unlike physical prisons, you can leave any time. Now is the time to break out of the cell of busyness and leave the valley of reactive living.

Follow me to freedom.

Follow me to the mountain top.

Dale Partridge

"The two most important days in your life are the day you are born and the day you find out why."

MARK TWAIN

DAY 01
It Comes At A Cost

You're talented. Maybe people have told you that before—a sports coach or your spouse or your parents. You're also passionate. People sense it in conversation with you around certain topics. Maybe friends have complimented how strong or driven or engaging you can be.

As you notice your talent, passion, and desire for success, you are wondering if you have a calling.

As I mentioned earlier, the answer is 'yes.' I know this because you're reading this book. Deep down in your gut, something big is stirring. You may not know where it comes from or what it wants you to do, but you can't deny that it exists. This almost divine dissatisfaction is triggered by—you guessed it—your calling. And the task before you is to not just discover it, but to live it.

If you have a pulse, you have a purpose. If you are breathing, you are meant for meaning. If you doubt whether you have a calling, you need only to believe three truths for now.

What you feel is normal. This stirring is universal among men. Every great male leader I've met tells me they feel a force drawing them forward. It's a sense of discontentment. A desire for largeness. A yearning for significance. Even when they don't have a name for this feeling, it propels them to keep moving when they want to quit. It is the fuel that ignites their deep sense of purpose. If you've felt this impulse to discover a larger purpose, you're not alone.

What you feel is positive. This impulse toward more doesn't mean you're inherently dissatisfied or psychologically imbalanced. It means you want to do something meaningful with your life. In fact, this yearning can be the catapult that propels you toward purpose. So don't resist this feeling; embrace it. The degree to which we listen to and act on the things which drive us determines how much fulfillment we will experience.

What you feel is impermanent. If the deep, hungry stirring makes you miserable, take hope. Millions of men have gone before you and they have broken through to the other side. You will not be purposeless forever. In order to move forward, you must believe this: Calling comes at a cost, and it's expensive. Not in dollars, but in emotional bandwidth.

Merriam-Webster defines a 'calling' as "a strong inner impulse toward a particular course of action especially when accompanied by conviction of divine influence." If you feel an inner impulse toward a new course of action, take a deep breath. The conviction of divine influence and a better life may be right around the corner.

ASK

When did I first notice a stirring to accomplish something more? Are there any associations I connect with this feeling that could shed more light on it?

_____

_____

_____

_____

_____

_____

_____

_____

_____

BELIEVE

My calling is expensive. I will make the payments with time, acute attentiveness, and emotional maturation.

DO   ☐ COMPLETED

Initiate an intentional 15-30 minute conversation about calling, and your journey to find yours, with your closest male friend.

"You're not lacking contentment if you want change; you're lacking contentment if you can't be happy while you wait for it."

UNKNOWN

DAY 02
Humans Love Rules

Humans love rules. Because a lot of us want others to remove the guesswork of living, we can allow others to tell us what to do. When we accept the rules of others, it allows us to escape the hard work of using discernment.

So, I'm sorry to tell you that there isn't an ironclad three-step process that you must follow to discover your calling. Instead, you must learn to navigate the mystery of it all.

And even though calling is a mystery, it isn't a complete mystery. It exists within a rough structure that can help guide us through the process of identifying what we're meant to do.

The framework begins with a counterintuitive principle: Calling is a singular word, but it is a plural principle. In other words, we often talk about 'calling,' but it might be more accurate to discuss 'callings.'

Primary Calling

Your primary calling is your heart's song. It's the song playing in your brain all the time. This is more than a job. It's more than a career path. It's more than a task list. Your primary calling is your life's soundtrack; the thoughts and actions that circle around it consume you.

Secondary Calling

Your secondary calling is your hand's work. It's the expression of your gifting that often occupies your time. You might get paid to live out your secondary calling, and it can change over time. It's an activity that may flow from your natural gifting and helps prepare you for your primary calling, yet it lives outside of its epicenter.

My friend Jonathan has a way with words. Actually, that's an understatement. He is a highly sought-after, world-class writer. His primary calling is to communicate truth by crafting beautiful prose. This is what wakes him up in the morning. It gives him purpose. When he is using words in this way, he feels alive.

Jonathan's primary calling is fulfilled in a variety of secondary callings. He has coached other writers, helped to craft business marketing copy, and has consulted with corporations and non-profits. He has written several books, ghostwritten dozens more, and has published thousands of columns and articles. Convinced that words change the world, his secondary calling has changed from season to season, but his heart continues to play the same song.

The first task in the journey toward your calling is to listen to your life. What is the song playing in the background throughout your day? Your calling is familiar, but it may not be obvious. So take time to reflect and listen for the melody. Do you hear it?

ASK

What do I love learning about, talking about, or teaching about?

_____

_____

_____

_____

_____

_____

BELIEVE

To fulfill my primary calling I must operate daily in my secondary calling.

DO   ☐ COMPLETED

List 5 possible career paths that require the use of your natural giftings.

_____

_____

_____

_____

_____

"Know yourself.
Because
you can't fix
something
you don't
understand."

UNKNOWN

DAY 03
Calling Never Compromises

Most leaders I know reveal that core values are important to their businesses. Most have defined them and many discuss them regularly in team meetings, but when I ask these leaders about their personal values, they often stammer, stutter, and grow silent. Just as a company cannot accomplish its mission without clearly understanding its values, so you cannot uncover your calling if you don't know what guides you.

One of the values I embrace is "Time beats money." Your bank account will rise and fall, but time is always slipping away. Job opportunities will come and go, but time only goes. Another value I hold dear is "People over profit." You may recognize it as the title of a book

I wrote. It's also a value that reminds me to always care more about how my business affects others than how much profit it turns.

What do you value more than anything else in life? What determines your moral code? What do you refuse to give up, no matter the stakes? What are your non-negotiables?

While you may be tempted to believe that your values are separate from your calling, the two are inextricably connected. Calling tends to flow from your beliefs and intersects with everything you do.

Your calling will complement rather than compete with your values and priorities.

For example, if you value healthy family relationships and your sense of 'calling' would weaken your relationships with them, you haven't identified it. If your 'calling' requires you to do harm to your reputation, then you need to rethink it. If your 'calling' leads you to take on an irresponsible amount of debt, then you have likely missed the mark.

Your calling should fit your life like a good pair of shoes. If you're a runner, you're not wearing boots; if you're a size nine, you're not sporting elevens. Sure, the right shoes may need to be broken in first—you might even have to use a shoehorn to slip them on—but ultimately they match up with your feet and where they're going. Resistance is healthy; incompatibility should be an alarm. You never need to compromise what you believe to live out what you were meant to do. And a man is more likely to compromise his values if he hasn't defined them yet.

ASK

What areas of my life do I believe are worth protecting
and why?

_____

_____

_____

_____

_____

BELIEVE

My calling will complement my values, not compromise
them.

DO   ☐ COMPLETED

Define your five personal core values. List them as short
phrases with one sentence to support each.

_____

_____

_____

_____

_____

_____

_____

"It's not hard to make decisions once you know what your values are."

ROY E. DISNEY

DAY 04

The Questions Behind
The Questions

Imagine that you have arrived home from a long day at the office and your wife asks, "What should we have for dinner?" You could respond to the question with whatever comes to your mind, but your answer is meaningless if you haven't answered other questions first.

For example you have to ask, "Which ingredients do we have?" You may want a pot roast, but if all you have is flour and sunflower seeds, don't waste time firing up the crockpot. You're not having roast. You also need to ask, "What food restrictions do we have?" If you make that pot roast for your vegetarian wife or bake a loaf of bread while you're on the Paleo diet, dinner isn't going to be a hit.

Some of the most mundane and the most significant questions in life are predicated on other questions. And so it is with your calling. That's why I always suggest that men who are searching for their calling begin by asking the questions behind the question. Here are three critical questions to answer before you'll ever discern your calling.

Do I believe in God?

Twentieth century author A.W. Tozer once said, "What comes into our minds when we think about God is the most important thing about us." He's right. And what you believe about God will influence what you think about calling: whether it exists, where it comes from, and what you must do to discover it. For some, the very question causes jaded skepticism and memories of unfortunate Sunday school experiences to bubble up in your gut. Don't skip this one. It must be defined by yes or no in order to move forward.

Do I want to be married?

If you want to live out your calling in society, you'll need to determine how you want to be engaged with society. The primary way most people throughout history have engaged with culture is through marriage and family. Of course, marriage isn't for everyone. But, historically and statistically, it's for most people. If you don't have a desire for marriage, you should ask yourself why. A firm yes or no answer to this question will help you be intentional about connecting to the world and others in distinct ways.

Do I want children?
Our modern culture paints the birth and rearing of children as being expensive and inconvenient. However, children and family become the entry point to maturity for many men. Children fuel the softer side of manhood and motivate many men to become providers and protectors of our homes. Take it from a father: it's tough work. Children will influence where you live, how you live, and what you can and can't do in any given season of life. But for men who want to grow up, kids are growth machines. They will transform you into a version of yourself you cannot develop any other way. You need to decide whether you're taking the journey or not.

Your life is largely a function of the clarity you've chosen for yourself. So, you need to determine not only the macro structure of your life—faith, marriage, children—but also the level of organizational clarity you desire. Next, you must embrace and cultivate the behaviors that prepare you for what you're meant to do.

You need to build a life that invites calling in.

It's difficult to invite calling into chaos. Do you still struggle to get up on time in the morning? Do you wrestle to keep your house clean? Do you run late to meetings or under-deliver on expectations? How can you expect to excavate your life's purpose while you're still a boy struggling with the basics of human responsibility?

You can't play in the yard if you won't get off the fence. And you can't live your calling if you refuse to make decisions. The recent generation's dilemmas of doubt, indecision, and fear of commitment will shipwreck your journey toward discovering your calling before it even begins. So, look in the mirror, grow up, and answer the questions behind the questions.

ASK

If something is holding me back from answering the three questions behind the questions, what is it? If not, what is it that keeps me committed to these choices?

_____

_____

_____

_____

_____

_____

_____

_____

_____

_____

BELIEVE

I can't find my calling until I find the answers to my life's biggest questions.

DO   ☐ COMPLETED

Set aside 60-90 minutes to evaluate these three questions. Do research if you need to, have an important conversation, or confront difficult thoughts. Stick with it until your answers leave you with a settled conviction on where you stand.

"The middle way
is no way."

ABIGAIL ADAMS

DAY 05
Let The Right Ones In

Most leaders think about calling as a personal decision that impacts their professional roles. That is, they assume that their calling is something they must discover alone and they think of it only as it relates to their jobs. We've already learned that calling is not just a professional matter. Today, we'll also notice that discerning it is not solely personal.

In the words of the poet John Donne, "No man is an island, entire of itself; every man is a piece of a continent, a part of the main." Even the strongest leaders must rely on those around them. This is true of almost every aspect of your life, especially your calling.

[1]

You don't get to do this alone. On this particular journey, independence is your enemy. Finding your calling requires intentional community and intense conversation. It requires safe people you've allowed to speak into your life.

Some of us would love to discover our calling in isolation so that we could walk into a room of people who matter to us and announce, "Here is my calling! I found it!" No. Calling is always connected to community. The search process requires the perspectives of others. If you have never discussed discerning your calling with those who know you best, this is your opportunity! Ask them where they see you excelling. Ask them where they recognize that which makes you come alive. Ask them where they notice your fiery passions finding expression. But most importantly, allow these people to provide an honest view of you as you navigate your voyage.

Because calling is not only professional, this process may get personal. What you're doing is a radical act of vulnerability. So the people you invite into this conversation matter. They need to be safe, wise, and committed to your flourishing. Ideally, they have history with you. In other words, don't ask your co-worker who you don't spend time with or the guy you met at the gym last month. If they haven't walked deeply with you before today, they shouldn't walk with you through this.

And because calling is both personal and professional, look for individuals who share similar giftings to yours. Consider people who have success in an area you'd like to explore. Find people whose life is ordered, settled, and directed. If you don't respect them both personally and professionally, their advice won't move you.

Your calling is not just about what's smart for you. It's about what's right for you.

Having the ability to determine the difference between what's smart—lucrative, career-advancing, ego-stroking—and what's right, the unique calling that has your name on it, is critical as you choose your team of advisors.

To make this even trickier, you must be capable of defining what 'right' is. For example, in philosophy, the word 'ought' has an implied moral authority. It suggests a universal right and wrong. In other words, phrases like 'should', 'ought', and 'right' are much weightier than we might realize.

I'm a Christian. That means the Bible is the foundational moral compass that guides me. I mention that to alert you to the need for a stable, unchanging ground from which you can determine 'right' and 'wrong.' As a great writer once said:

"When the storm has swept by, the unfounded are gone but the firm stand forever." - Proverbs 10:25

There are plenty of worthy paths on the journey to discern your calling. There are many smart people to help you find the way, but in order to discover the right path, you'll need to surround yourself with the right people. You'll need to know what 'right' truly is. It's a deep question, and a critical one. Calling can't be discovered by a man who has a moving target of morality.

ASK

How do I determine right and wrong? Is it my government, my culture, my faith, or something else? Does it ever change? If so, why?

_____

_____

_____

_____

_____

_____

_____

BELIEVE

My calling is found through right thinking, not smart thinking.

DO   □ COMPLETED

List 1 to 3 safe, right people you'll ask for outside perspective this week.

_____

_____

_____

_____

"Just because
something is
smart, doesn't
mean it's right."

UNKNOWN

DAY 06
Own It

I've mentioned the importance of making wise choices in this process, but calling requires both choices and change. And change is where most men get stuck.

A few days ago, we discussed the three questions to answer before tackling the other questions. If you believe in God, what changes? If you want to be married, what changes? If you want to have kids, what changes?

Change is derived from a shift in thinking. New thinking results in new behaviors. New behaviors produce different outcomes.

Backing up a bit, these changes are behaviors that are often identified more commonly as: personal habits, discipline, routine, and schedule. These are where clarity begins. They're where your life comes into focus.

A few years ago, after being challenged by my friend, I decided to stop flying by the seat of my pants. I killed busy. I assassinated adolescence. I stayed in one place where people could finally know me, grow me, and show me who I was. I created an almost fanatical structured daily routine that allowed me to discover who I was. I protected time for important reading to stimulate my thinking.

The less time I spent wondering what to do with my day, the more time I had to determine what I could do with my life.

The process of finding our callings isn't all that complicated. We make it complicated because of our fear to commit to the things we've said we will do, follow the direction we know we should go, and embrace the life we have chosen to create. A called leader will not allow fear of overcoming the discrepancy between who he is now and who he is meant to become to hinder him.

So, beat back the procrastination, clarify what two or three major things must change, and implement the necessary habits and structure that will allow your calling to reveal itself to you.

ASK

What two or three major things in my life need to change to welcome calling into my life?

_____

_____

_____

_____

_____

_____

BELIEVE

Choices and change are different. My calling requires both.

DO   ☐ COMPLETED

From your answers above, list the daily habits or routine adjustments you will make to support these changes.

_____

_____

_____

_____

_____

_____

"You can't change what's going on around you until you change what's going on within you."

ZIG ZIGLAR

#FindYourCalling

DAY 07
The Career Of Calling

'Calling' has been so overused in recent years that it has morphed into something of a catch-all junk drawer for how we spend our time. Do you like to knit? Great, that's your calling. Do you sell insurance to make ends meet? Excellent, you've found your calling! Have you been in telecommunications for 25 years? Fantastic, that must be your calling.

To be honest, most of us have a better idea of what we don't want in a job than what we do want. We don't want something mundane. We don't want anything similar to the work of our parents who turned wrenches or answered phones. And we certainly don't want anything with a two-hour commute. After all, a third of our lives will be spent working. We'll probably spend more time at work than we do with our spouses and kids. It's no wonder we agonize over 'what to be when we grow up.'

We want a job that doesn't actually feel like a job. We hunger for something that uses our talents and brings us great satisfaction. What we really want isn't a job at all; we want a calling.

In order to understand what your calling is, you'll need to recognize what your calling is not. So, let's identify and eliminate four competing concepts that are not synonymous with calling.

Hobby

A hobby is something you do because you enjoy it. Or because it fascinates you. Perhaps you do it because it just passes the time. Hobbies don't stress you out. Typically, they relax you. Maybe you like to play golf or tennis, or maybe you're a fitness freak who goes to the gym three hours a day. Or perhaps you like to scrapbook. (I don't know why anyone would like to do this, but I'm told that many do.) You rarely get paid for your hobby, and if you do, it usually ceases to be a hobby.

Job

Unless you're a Hilton or a Trump, you're going to have

to have a job. This is what pays the bills. You may or may not enjoy it. You may or may not be paid well to do it, but you have this job because it allows you to survive in a capitalistic society. When you leave your job for the day, you usually stop thinking about it unless you're lucky enough to have a overbearing boss (I'm kidding). In today's marketplace, few jobs offer lasting security and stability. In fact, yours will likely change 15 to 20 times in your lifetime. [2]

Career
Career is the word most commonly used to describe the long arc of someone's employment. The word "career" derives from the medieval Latin word *carraria*, which means "road for vehicles." This is the path you take through a series of jobs over time and it is usually associated with a single occupation. If you're in your thirties or older, you're likely on a career path by now.

Calling
Calling is often used interchangeably with vocation, which comes from the Latin word meaning "to call." Your calling is the pursuit that gives you meaning. It's the rumble in your gut. It's the way you would orient your life to accomplish what matters most if you found out you had a terminal illness. I wish I'd heard when I was younger that one's calling is not something to be magically revealed, but is something to be recognized.

You have to listen for it. You have to search for it. You have to discover it, even as it discovers you. Of the four ways to think about how you glean meaning and purpose and sustenance, calling is the only one that you can expect to remain consistent over a lifetime.

When it comes to lasting satisfaction and happiness, those who occupy themselves with hobbies and jobs are the least satisfied. Those who pursue career and calling feel the most satisfied.[3] No surprises there. As I've clarified, your calling encompasses more than the work you are paid for; it taps into your whole life purpose. When you've found your calling, you experience satisfaction and genuine fulfillment. Conversely, if you're living a life at odds with your vocation, the fruitlessness of that choice will be evident as well. You may be indescribably restless. Or maybe you wake up in the middle of the night feeling like you can't breathe. Life may seem to be passing you by.

Unfortunately, as we get older, our true selves can get lost among the influences and expectations of family, friends, teachers, and the media. In school and in society we get sorted and placed into labeled slots. Instead of listening to the call within us, we begin to make decisions based on our need for approval, prestige, and security.

Embracing your calling means rejecting the misguided

voices of others and choosing to live authentically. It means refusing to blindly imitate dad or other men you admire. Too often we heed every voice, influence, and belief except our own. We drink up what our teachers tell us, what our parents tell us, what our ministers tell us, and what other wise sages have spoken and written. We make these sources of truth authoritative, but we dismiss our own insights and understanding as hopelessly irrelevant.[4]

Your hobbies won't likely stem from your calling. Your job may not be connected to your calling. Your career may not be an extension of your calling, but, ideally, that's the goal. If you've been confusing your calling with its cousins, it's time to change your thinking. If you can, you'll be one step closer to discovering what you were meant to do.

ASK

Is my job supporting my passions or smothering them? What changes can I make this month that will help develop me for what I'm meant to do?

_____

_____

_____

_____

_____

BELIEVE

I can't discover my calling if I confuse it with career.

DO   ☐ COMPLETED

List your hobbies, your job, and your career path. Then draft a description of what you're beginning to discern that your calling might be.

_____

_____

_____

_____

_____

_____

_____

"The deepest
vocational
question is not
'What ought I to
do with my life?'
It is the more
demanding 'Who
am I? What is my
nature?"

PARKER J. PALMER

#FindYourCalling

DAY 08
Calling Is Never For You

Most men have a 'me'-centric, or myopic, understanding of calling. They believe that finding their calling will make them more fulfilled, more productive, more successful, more happy and more wealthy. They don't give much thought to how others could and should be affected.

On the journey to unearth my calling, I founded an ecommerce company with a simple mission. We sold high-quality goods and donated a portion of each purchase to a charitable organization. Honestly, I was enjoying myself and felt the work I was doing had propelled me closer to what I was meant to do. One day a friend of mine noticed the good our organization had accomplished and mused, "Dang, Dale. Imagine if you didn't start this company."

His comment was a simple observation, but it struck a nerve for me. For the first time, I considered all the people whose lives would have been different if I'd chosen to say 'no' to this dream. If I had chosen to avoid this pursuit I felt called to, it's possible that thousands of people might have died. Because our business funded fresh water wells, fed hungry children, and provided shelter to those in need, the millions of dollars we raised had very palpable life and death consequences.

Your calling is always about others.

You might not be feeding starving children, but your calling still impacts others. You might not be giving shelter to the poor, but you may be solving a cultural dilemma, bringing people together, or inventing the solution to a problem deeply impacting the lives of others. Your willingness, your excellence, and your courage will touch many lives beyond your own. You may experience pleasure as you embrace your calling, but it will certainly also benefit others. Not living it isn't just a disservice to you, but is also a disservice to those you're intended to serve.

So, while your calling is based on your giftedness, desires, and affirmations, it will always build the story of another for the purpose of benefiting the other. As author Frederick Buechner once said, "The place God calls you to is the place where your deep gladness and the world's deep hunger meet." [5] As you consider your internal sense of calling, also consider its external effects. As you consider others in this process, you might just discover that your calling can satisfy a great hunger that's not your own.

ASK

How has my work benefitted others in the past? Is there a connection between what I did and how others were affected?

_____

_____

_____

_____

BELIEVE

My calling isn't for me; it's for them.

DO   ☐ COMPLETED

In order of impact, list 2-3 of your passions that offer the greatest benefit to others. Then explain the value those people will experience.

_____

_____

_____

_____

_____

_____

_____

"Shift your efforts from making a million dollars to helping a million people."

DHARMESH SHAH

DAY 09
Calling Is Close To Home

My friend Charles has never met a calling he didn't like. He's so enthusiastic about life and work and serving that after talking to anyone for five minutes, he can be convinced that their calling must be his, too.

Many men can take this approach to business. If their best friend has a strong sense of leadership, they end up mimicking it. If their father founded a business, they may do the same. While this can sometimes work out, calling must be profoundly connected to one's own talents and gifts.

Where do you excel? What gives you energy? Which skills do you possess in greater measure than most others you know? Gifts and talents are interconnected, but they are not interchangeable. Knowing the difference between the two will help you determine which of each you posses.

Talents are skills that you inherit. They come from either your parents or your extended gene pool. We probably all know someone who comes from a family with natural abilities in a particular area. Think of the Manning family in the NFL. Or consider the Kardashians. Okay, maybe that wasn't the best example, but you get the point. Talents are those innate skills so prominent in a family lineage that if someone doesn't have them, others may remark, "Oh, didn't get the (fill-in-the-blank) gene."

Gifts are skills that you acquire. Like any present, a gift is received. For us spiritual folks, they're those skills you received divinely. But more commonly, gifts are often a result of environment. You became great at math because the schools you attended had excellent math teachers who nurtured your interests. Or you had the opportunity to excel in a certain sport because you were born into a culture that valued athletics.

Everyone has innate talents and acquired gifts. This doesn't mean you're better at these things than anyone else, only that you possess these skills in abundance. Some of your gifts and talents are readily apparent.

Others are seeds requiring fertilization, watering, and pruning. Some are valued by the culture you live in, and others that may be just as important, aren't.

As you look at your genetics and your environment, notice your talents and gifts. And then ask the big question: "How might these skills shed light on what I am meant to do?"

ASK

Based on what I've seen and others have told me, what are my three most evident talents and gifts?

_____

_____

_____

_____

BELIEVE

My calling will be carried out by my natural gifting.

DO   ☐ COMPLETED

For each of your top three talents and gifts written above, list 3 industries or causes or areas of need where they could be utilized.

_____

_____

_____

_____

_____

_____

_____

"Remember who you were before the world told you who you should be."

DANIELLE LAPORTE

#FindYourCalling

DAY 10
Remember Who You Are

Messages matter. What your parents, your teachers, your friends, your wife, or the broader culture have told you, and are still telling you, will shape your beliefs about yourself. Too often leaders can't hear their heart's song because there's so much noise being trumpeted by others. Today, we're going to attack three common lies of confusion and coercion that impacted the boy you used to be.

"You can't be that." Who has spoken discouragement into your life? Who spoke a 'can't' over you that haunts you at night? Maybe they've called it a 'family curse' or have told you "that's just how we [enter last name] s are." For example, when we were kids, my friend's dad told him he was lazy all the time, and now he's convinced he is. It doesn't matter that he works two full-time jobs. He is literally killing himself to prove that he isn't lazy. I also remember my teacher continually telling one of the troublemakers in the class that he "would never amount to anything." I wonder if he is living out her words today. I expect he might be. As the Bible says, "Train a child up in the way that he should go, and they will not depart from it." (Proverbs 22:6) If you were raised with courage you'll seize opportunities. If you were trained to question yourself, you'll do that, too. All around us are men fulfilling the messages they heard when they were being raised. Are you?

"You should be that." Are you living out someone else's dream? My friend is an immigrant from a culture that encourages children to pursue 'respectable' careers like being physicians or lawyers. Today she is a doctor, but I often wonder what she'd be doing if her parents hadn't pushed her into that field. I received an email recently from a guy who took over his father's mechanic shop even though he is an artist at heart. How many people are stuck because of the shoulds that have been spoken over them?

"You were not meant to be that." Often your calling is the very thing you've been told by someone else you can't do or would never be. You'll need to identify these comments and examine their validity. On the flip side,

I've seen men who are far too impressionable. They assume their calling is simply what someone else has told them it is.

In order to discover your calling, you'll need to develop the discernment to evaluate your options objectively.

Finding out what we're meant to do is a beautiful mess. But to put it in the words of my mentor, "Remember who you were before the world told you who you should be. Remind yourself of who you were before the world told you who you can't be. And in that place is where you'll find who you are called to be."

ASK

What harmful messages have the people from my past
told me? How have they affected my thinking?

_____

_____

_____

_____

BELIEVE

If I believe a lie, it will negatively affect my life.

DO   ☐ COMPLETED

Take five minutes to remind yourself who you are.
Below, write down as many true things about your
personality as you can think of. Start with "I am…"

_____

_____

_____

_____

_____

_____

_____

_____

"If you think wrong, you'll never live strong."

MATTHEW L. JACOBSON

DAY 11
Asking The Right Questions

When it comes to calling, where you start will influence how you finish. Think of an Olympic race. You can have the most ballin' shoes and the flashiest gear and even lightning fast legs, but if you're starting 200 meters behind the other runners, it won't matter.

Unfortunately, the way many popular leaders have talked about calling hasn't been helpful. They've thrown out slick clichés that don't help us move any closer to discovering what we were meant to do. They're simply shadows of the classic childhood question, "What do you want to be when you grow up?" My guess is that you've heard, repeated, or pondered one or two of these poorly crafted questions yourself, so let's unravel a few of them.

Incorrect Question: "If money were no object, what would you do?"

This one is so unrealistic, I'm surprised so many people suggest it. Starting with "if money were no object" is like starting with "if you didn't have to breathe air." It's not realistic because money will always be an object. If I, as a husband and father, start acting like money doesn't matter, I'll end up in a world of trouble. While we should fear the temptations that come from excess money, as well as the perils of poverty, we can't pretend that money doesn't matter.

Correct Question: If you could choose a calling that would fuel your passions and provide for your family, what would you do?

Incorrect Question: "If you could guarantee that you wouldn't fail, what would you attempt?"

The first problem with this query is the same as the last one. You can't guarantee you will not fail. If you're willing to try something new, failure will always be a possibility. If you're 45-years-old and want to leave your sales job to play Major League Baseball, it isn't going to happen. Every man should consider the real possibility of failure before handing in our two-week notice. At the same time, this posture assumes that failure is negative. But failure can also grow us, show us, and at times direct us toward our calling.

Correct Question: Despite the possibility of failure, what are you willing to take a risk on?

Incorrect Question: "If you could do anything, what would make you happy?"

The problem with this is that it assumes that whatever makes you happy must be good for you. If sex makes you happy, then you might as well cheat on your wife to have more of it. If money makes you happy, then you'll feel validated in your greed. Rather than ask what makes us happy and pursue it blindly, we should ask whether the things that make us happy should make us happy. Yes, our callings should offer fulfillment and happiness. But just because something makes you happy, doesn't mean it qualifies as a 'calling'.

Correct Question: Of the things that make you happy, which are the ones that make you whole?

ASK

How can I avoid faulty arguments that can muddy my discernment about my calling?

_____

_____

_____

_____

BELIEVE

I will direct my life with wisdom, rather than through cliché aphorisms.

DO   ☐ COMPLETED

Answer the three 'correct' questions.

_____

_____

_____

_____

_____

_____

_____

_____

"The art of being wise is the art of knowing what to overlook."

WILLIAM JAMES

#FindYourCalling

DAY 12
The Oversaturated Calling

One of the greatest threats to your calling can be your fascination with someone else's. Too many people begin to explore their callings and then balk after realizing they aren't the only one who has it.

"Too many people do this," they say. "I'll never be better than the rest."

I struggled with this feeling when I decided to live out part of my calling by writing a book. I looked at the marketplace and saw other books on business, leadership, and entrepreneurship. A voice in my head whispered that the need was already met and I was wasting my time. The voice told me that the other authors were better than me and that the finish line had already been crossed. Why should someone like me write a book when so many people have already written others? Who did I think I was?

In an environment where men are evaluated on our performance—where we're expected to succeed, rewarded for results, and scolded for mistakes—the search for our calling is a prime breeding ground for fear, anxiety, and shame. So, we must deal with the internal voices that give these a foothold in our heart and minds. Three truths have helped me dispel these obstacles on my journey toward a life of purpose.

1.Fear kills calling more than failure ever will.
The path to your calling is often walked with weak knees. Everyone has a fear of failure, but many also have a fear of success. What will happen if your business takes off, if your dream materializes, if your book becomes a bestseller? How will you survive that level of responsibility? Do you possess the capacity, talent, and guts to operate at a higher level? Ultimately, the fear that you can't sustain your calling or survive it will often rob you of the joy of discovering it.

2. The middle road is a dead end street.
Discovering your calling requires making critical decisions. Yet many leaders are racked with indecision, and this creates anxiety. My friend was recently faced

with a possible company merger, but he couldn't make up his mind about whether to move forward. So, instead of making a decision, he sat on it. For months, he languished in indecision. I finally told him that either decision would be better than living with no decision. Taking the middle road had led him nowhere.

Many leaders experience 'paralysis by analysis' when they overthink a situation to the point where they end up stuck. We often assume that pausing to consider our options is a better strategy than moving forward and choosing the wrong option, but this is only true to a point. This approach eventually leads to more stress, more worry, and less serenity. Peace is found in moving, not standing still.

3. Yes, you're worthy.

When men catch a whiff of our calling, we begin to imagine how living it out will change our lives. And when the vision is better than our existing situation, we might not believe we deserve it. Bestselling author Brené Brown says, "Shame—the intensely painful feeling or experience of believing that we are flawed and therefore unworthy of love and belonging—breeds fear." [6]

Some men have allowed their past to teach them that they don't deserve purpose. So they self-sabotage to prove that what they've accepted is true. Others were raised in a *quid pro quo* culture that makes them think they need to work overtime to earn whatever they get. So they self-inflict enough pain to make them feel as though they're entitled to whatever purpose they can glean.

These three barriers—fear, worry, and shame—are internal, not external. Unfortunately, it's much easier to overcome external obstacles than inner obstacles. Notice these three and scrap them. Calling is free, and everyone—including you—deserves to live with purpose.

ASK

Have I adopted patterns of faulty thinking? If so, where is the root and what can I do to begin the process of healing?

_____

_____

_____

_____

BELIEVE

I find my calling when I fix my thinking.

DO   ☐ COMPLETED

List three personal qualities of strength that will aid you in combating doubt and thinking clearly. Next, list three qualities you've not yet mastered but desire to embody.

_____

_____

_____

_____

_____

_____

"A healthy outside starts from the inside."

ROBERT URICH

DAY 13
Don't Run So Fast You Leave Yourself Behind

Few moments annoy a father more than when one of their children shouts from the back of the minivan, "Are we there yet?" But some of us act the same way in life and business. Once an idea strikes, we want the final product as soon as possible. We want to act immediately, see results, cross the finish line. We don't want to take a road trip in a minivan; we want to push a button on a teleporter.

Many leaders even celebrate haste. They brag about how aggressive they are, dubbing themselves "go-getters." This rationalization is just an attempt to rename a flaw as an asset. Unfortunately, it can short-circuit a journey toward purpose. These men confuse impatience with persistence. They fail to value and utilize the time between inspiration and realization as a critical period for preparation.

The value of this principle has been deeply ingrained in some of my Jewish friends. They grew up hearing about Moses spending 40 years waiting in the wilderness. They're familiar with the story of King David being called as a boy to lead, but waiting years to serve. They know the story of Daniel who spent nearly a decade serving a pagan king before his famous lions' den moment. As a Christian, I also value the wisdom of waiting. Jesus waited 30 years before launching his ministry and the Apostle Paul spent prep time in the desert after discovering his calling and before living it out.

Though it's natural to wish for immediate results like Jack and his magical beanstalk, you're not Jack and your calling isn't a beanstalk. If you've recently planted the seed in the ground, don't expect a tree to germinate, sprout, and grow overnight. Plan, instead, to work for your calling and wait for your timing. Patience isn't just a torture device; it's a shaping tool. The discipline of waiting is one of the overlooked tools that men can wield.

ASK

What role has patience played in my life? Is waiting for the long-term vision difficult for me? What will help me to patiently endure the time between inspiration and realization?

_____

_____

_____

_____

_____

_____

_____

_____

BELIEVE

The time between now and the realization of my life's work is the most important season of my life.

DO   ☐ COMPLETED

Look up one of history's great leaders whose life inspires you, and find their biography. Whether it's the short or long version, read it. Take your time and notice the richness of the timeline, not the rush to the finish line.

"Passion is the willingness to suffer for something you love."

UNKNOWN

#FindYourCalling

DAY 14
Misery Loves Company

When I hosted bestselling author Ken Blanchard on my StartupCamp.com podcast, I asked him what advice he would give his 18-year-old self. He offered, "Don't let anyone tell you what you're supposed to do."

When Ken was a young man, he was told he couldn't write and that he should go into college administration. Naïvely he believed this advice and became an administrative dean in Southern California. He wasn't good at administration, but he'd acted on the advice he'd been given. Years later, a friend asked him to co-write a book. He didn't think he was up to the task, but reluctantly agreed. To his surprise, the book was a wild success. The unexpected success became an opportunity for him to self-correct. Today, Ken Blanchard has produced more than 60 books that have sold nearly 20 million copies!

As you discern your calling, others will weigh in. Hear everyone, but only listen to a few.

People are wired to pursue calling. They want to discover it and may be frustrated if they haven't found it. So, some may be jealous when they witness you searching for yours or living it out. Although everyone has a specific purpose in this life, insecurity persuades people to behave otherwise.

The advice some offer may not be he helpful. It might not sound malicious. It might not be very far off base. It might even come from a well-meaning place. But their words won't always align with what you're discovering to be true about yourself. When you notice the tension of this misalignment, exercise caution. Misery loves company, but you don't have to join the party.

Imagine what your life would look like if you always listened to what people said about who you were supposed to be or what you were supposed to do. Some advice may have been useful; other words would be better ignored.

Be willing to plug in, listen, and notice what's motivated

by love, wisdom, jealousy, or brokenness. As you exercise discernment, you'll learn to recognize the truth when you hear it.

ASK

Who comes to mind when I think of the people that truly want the best for me? How have they proven they are worth listening to?

_____

_____

_____

_____

BELIEVE

Just because something sounds smart to me doesn't mean it's right for me.

DO   ☐ COMPLETED

List three non-negotiable traits that qualify someone to speak into your journey to discover your calling.

_____

_____

_____

_____

_____

_____

_____

"Discernment is the ability to see things for what they really are, not for what you want them to be."

UNKNOWN

DAY 15
Clearly Uncomfortable

Think about a moment in your life when your future was guaranteed. Keep thinking. Don't stop. Just one time. A single moment. Do you have it in your mind? I didn't think so. Your good health could evaporate tomorrow. The stock market could crash and wipe away your nest egg. Your wife could be involved in an accident, a loved one could tragically pass away, or your house could burn down.

Uncertainty makes us uncomfortable. When we're missing information, or when we anticipate the possibility of danger, uncertainty elicits caution. Humans naturally resist it. We plan for the future, prepare for the future, and save for the future. Yet as hard as we work hard to minimize uncertainty, we'll never eliminate it. Accepting this reality is critical to discovering what we were meant to do.

Discovering your calling requires stepping into the unknown. Walking into mystery. Relinquishing control. If ambiguous situations make you step back or shut down, you'll fail to discover your purpose. Uncertainty is a prerequisite of calling and allowing that discomfort requires courage.

Though some may see ambiguity as a liability, it can actually be an opportunity. As pastor and author Andy Stanley says, "Where there is no uncertainty, there is no longer the need for leadership. The greater the uncertainty, the greater the need for leadership. Your capacity as a leader will be determined by how well you learn to deal with uncertainty." [7]

As men who are the leaders of our lives, we can be uncertain, but we shouldn't be indecisive. If you make a bad decision, people will forgive you and you can forgive yourself. But if you cannot make a decision, no one will follow you and you will begin to distrust your own ability to lead. So, you must learn to walk with confidence into uncertain seasons of your life. There's no way to predict what you'll discover as you search for your purpose, but you can hold your head high and stand strong while you seek it out. You might not know the curve of every trail, but you can be confident that you're climbing the right mountain.

ASK

On this journey toward clarity, what scares me?

_____

_____

_____

_____

BELIEVE

Sometimes my only option for moving forward is a leap of faith.

DO   ☐ COMPLETED

List three elements of your calling about which you currently have clarity. Next, list three elements of your calling about which you feel uncertain.

_____

_____

_____

_____

_____

_____

_____

_____

"In any given moment we have two options: to step forward into growth or to step back into safety."

ABRAHAM MASLOW

DAY 16
Let Your Life Do The Preaching

As you begin to discover your calling, you might feel a sense of pride in what you've accomplished. You know that what you're discovering matters deeply. You're convinced that your life will never be the same. And you want to tell the world about what you've found. Don't let your sense of pride make you prideful. Resist the temptation to brag about your calling.

The ancient Chinese philosopher Lao Tzu once said,

"I have three precious things which I hold fast and prize. The first is gentleness; the second is frugality; the third is humility, which keeps me from putting myself before others. Be gentle and you can be bold; be frugal and you

can be liberal; avoid putting yourself before others and
you can become a leader among men." [8]

While it sounds counterintuitive, being humble in your
calling is the key to living your calling with boldness.

Just like you, I've felt the temptation to become prideful
and overshare the insights I'm gleaning about the nature
of my calling, but here are three ways I've found to
responsibly resist that urge.

1. Accept the process.
Unwrapping my calling has been like reading a book.
I glimpsed the first page years ago, but that's all there
was. It contained enough content that I knew what
kind of book I was reading and the direction the story
was headed, but I didn't know how the narrative would
unfold. Conversations, life-lessons, and relationships
since then have revealed additional sentences,
paragraphs, and pages. By the time I'm an old man, and
my beard has turned grey, I'll finally have access to the
entire book. As you realize and accept that calling is a
process, and that you are not the one writing the book,
you'll live into and speak about your calling with more
humility.

2. Don't declare your calling; display it.
Don't be that guy who deciphers his calling, prints the
business cards and acquires the domain name without

any input or affirmation from others. That guy believes he's the gift the world needs and lets everyone else know exactly what he will and won't do. Instead, simply go out and use your gift. Let people see your calling. Let people affirm your calling. Organic affirmation from a variety of sources over a long stretch of time might be the most powerful assurance one can receive. Here's the uncomfortable truth: if nobody agrees or affirms it, then it's likely not your calling. If everyone else affirms it, because you're faithfully living it out, then you won't have to do the excruciating work of convincing them.

3. Release your expectations.
I've addressed overcoming your fears and others' expectations for your journey. However, the challenge in this part of the process is relinquishing your own expectations. In a world where everyone gets a trophy and we're inundated with messages about how special we are, most of us expect to be the heroes of our own lives. We expect to win. We expect to conquer. We expect to have the spotlight shining brightly on our work. Release the expectation you have to be the hero of every scene. Your calling makes you the world's servant, not the world's savior.

ASK

When I think of a humble yet confident man, what character traits come to mind?

_____

_____

_____

_____

_____

_____

BELIEVE

Humility isn't denying my strengths; it's embracing my weaknesses.

DO   ☐ COMPLETED

List three ways you can show your community your calling without telling them your calling.

_____

_____

_____

_____

_____

_____

_____

"You are what you do, not what you'll say you'll do."

CARL GUSTAV JUNG

#FindYourCalling

DAY 17
Pick a Road and Go

Men often use the phrase "the road less traveled" to describe blazing a courageous path or making a difficult decision. The phrase comes from a Robert Frost poem and most people overlook an important detail. The narrator looks at two paths and notes that the more traveled road looked "just as fair." In other words, both roads had their strengths and weakness, their positives and negatives, their pros and cons. One path seemed to be as good of an option as the other.

This is where most of us live when it comes to our callings. We see two possible paths forward that seem good enough. Maybe more. We have the gifts and talents and passions that would allow us to succeed in any of the several paths before us.

Maybe you're sitting at your kitchen table with your mind maps, questionnaires, index cards and post-it notes spread out in front of you. You're wondering how you're supposed to choose a path with all of this information available to you. Which road should you travel, and how should you choose?

I once heard brilliance defined as "making something complex seem simple." So, begin by narrowing your options. Options can be a blessing, but can also be a burden. To succeed, you need to winnow down your possibilities to a manageable number of options. I suggest forcing yourself to release all but three. Keep them broad. Don't write that you want to start a summer camp; write that you want to work with youth. Don't write the name and mission statement of the non-profit you want to start; write that you want to give the world clean water.

To discern among the three, you'll need to use your intuition. Also, consider consulting some of your wisest confidants.

I'm not asking you to choose a calling just yet, but to move in that direction sort your thinking into categories by using this guide:

1. List what you've discerned as your top 3 callings. (Yes, literally write them down.)

2. Add one sentence about why each direction excites you. What would you be saying "yes" to?

3. Add another sentence about what you would be saying 'no' to if you choose a particular direction.

You may only need to follow this three-step process once to make a selection. You might try it and know that you know. But you might complete it and still feel torn. In this case, you may need to spend time thinking and praying and discerning. Or perhaps you'll need to give yourself permission to test one and see what happens. It's okay if you spend time pursuing your sense of a calling that doesn't pan out. And it's also okay that you choose not to travel every possible road. Don't worry about choosing the road least traveled; discover and take the one you feel called to walk.

ASK

Do I typically go with the flow or pave my own way?
Why do I do this?

_____

_____

_____

_____

BELIEVE

If I want to be extraordinary I must eliminate the
unnecessary.

DO   ☐ COMPLETED

Complete the exercise found in today's lesson.

_____

_____

_____

_____

_____

_____

_____

_____

"The choices we make lead up to actual experiences. It is one thing to decide to climb a mountain. It is quite another to be on top of it."

HERBERT A. SIMON

DAY 18
The Right of Passage

When leaders want to grow, they usually seek noise. They listen to a podcast or have a conversation with a like-minded friend or hire a coach to offer advice. Or maybe they read a book, which is visual noise that stimulates the brain like an audible voice.

While all of these growth techniques can be useful, sometimes we need to quiet our hearts and minds to learn through silence.

Up until now in this process, you've been receiving and processing information to clarify your calling. You've synthesized wisdom and advice through the questions and exercises in these pages. You've had vulnerable conversations in community. And you've explored the nuances of your gifts and talents. Now it's time to shut up and ship out.

Science is now revealing that silence is even more beneficial for human bodies and minds than we once assumed. A few minutes of silence can increase your blood circulation, lower your blood pressure, and promote brain cell production. You're actually more creative right after periods of silence, which is why you may get a spark of genius in the middle of the night. People who spend time in silence have lower rates of depression and anxiety. They also have longer attention spans. While you may think silence is a waste of your time, it may be one of the best ways you can spend your time.

The moment you decide to commit to your calling is a monumental one. To prepare for it, I'm asking you to enter a period of intentional quiet time to clarify your thoughts and steady your sea legs. For some, it might mean a trip to the mountains. For others it might be a day at the beach. Someone else might hole up in a friend's home while they're away. Whatever you choose here are a few ground rules for your pause trip:

• Retreat for at least 24 hours. Jesus took 40 days and nights. If you can't set aside one day, then you're not ready to live this out.

• Relinquish technology. Your phone and laptop need to stay shut down. And, I'm sorry, but you'll have to miss The Tonight Show. No television. You have to disconnect to reconnect.

• Get outside if possible. Humans are meant to connect with nature. It is our natural habitat. So, leave the phosphorescent glow of your home and explore the outdoors.

• Choose a quiet place. It could be a cabin, a cottage or maybe just a hotel room. But it must be quiet.

During your getaway, spend as much time in quiet as possible. Think. Pray. Journal. Daydream. Clear the distractions so that you can discover for yourself:

You are not stuck.
You are moving forward.
You don't yet know how you'll get there.
You're doing the necessary hard work to figure it out.
You're ready to accept your calling and live what you were meant to do.

ASK

Where does my best thinking occur? How can I integrate this into my pause trip?

_____

_____

_____

_____

BELIEVE

Silence is an important ingredient to discover my calling.

DO   ☐ COMPLETED

Schedule the date for your pause trip and fill in the details below.

_____

_____

_____

_____

_____

_____

_____

_____

"Thousands of tired, nerve-shaken, over-civilized people are beginning to find out that going to the mountains is going home; that wildness is a necessity."

JOHN MUIR

DAY 19
Breaking Ground

What makes you feel most afraid? For me, the list definitely includes bears. Those brown, hairy murderers are pure evil. I sometimes think that hell isn't fiery at all. It's just a giant cage with nothing inside but a bad person and a bear. Seriously.

Among the list of most men's greatest worries is the fear of making a bad decision. What if you hire the wrong person? Or what if you fire the wrong person? What if you miscalculate a financial decision that puts your family at risk? These are types of questions that keep men up at night, but not making a decision is far more dangerous than making a wrong decision.

At this point in the journey to discover and embrace your calling, you have enough information to determine what you were meant to do. You've thought about it, prayed about it, and talked to others about it. You've made lists and taken inventory. You've been wise, patient, and thorough. If you've still not been able to determine at least the general direction, fear is what's holding you back or slowing you down.

This is the moment to notice what your default behavior is. Are you always playing it safe? Are you too impulsive? Do you procrastinate? Notice whether there might be a persistent behavior hindering your journey. Ask those around you what hampers your ability to make a confident decision. Call it out, let it go, and move forward.

If this advice seems simplistic, it is. Once you've done all the necessary work needed to make a good choice, nothing is left to do but to make it. If you are too fearful to inch forward, you'll have to release that fear before you can move on. If you refuse to release it, you'll stay stuck. At this point, no one can help you except you. Only you can overcome the paralysis that's kept you stuck.

Accepting a calling doesn't mean you've forever sealed your fate. Be open to change, but commit to move in the direction you've chosen. You'll evolve over time, just like a sapling that becomes a tree. But you'll need to emerge from the ground in order to begin the process. You can't start growing until you get going.

ASK

What's stopped me, in the past, from making big decisions? Are those same elements at play here?

_____

_____

_____

BELIEVE

I won't fear the consequence of my choice more than the result of not choosing at all.

DO   ☐ COMPLETED

Produce the first draft of your calling in words.
I'm called to: [1-3 sentence version]
I'm called to: [Five words or less version.]

_____

_____

_____

_____

_____

_____

_____

_____

"You are one decision away from a totally different life."

MARK BATTERSON

DAY 20
Passion, Meet Preparation

You're getting ready to launch into one of life's great adventures. So, you might be thinking that you need a little bit of luck right about now. Should you purchase a rabbit's foot? Ask your pastor to anoint you with special oil? Eat a bowl of Lucky Charms? (They are magically delicious, after all.)

I don't know that any of these steps are necessary. As entrepreneur and bestselling author Jack Canfield has said, "People make their own luck by great preparation and good strategy." Show me the luckiest business leader who changed the world, and I'll show you a prepared leader with a solid strategy.

What do you need to do in order to fully embrace your calling? Some will need to create a spreadsheet of items to purchase. Others need to down a list of pros and cons. Some need to have some more conversations with trusted advisors. Others may need to write letters to themselves. And others may need to enlist professional assistance to help them move forward.

No matter who you are, you need to draft a plan. As with drafting a business plan, many people assume that this process is for the benefit of others. But this is actually for you. While your day of silence equipped your heart, drafting your plan will equip your head. Passion is helpful, but so is preparation.

Let's start with a two-page calling overview. This will be the final document that defines your calling, and it is the proof—to yourself and to others—that you've done your homework before moving forward.

Two-page calling overview

1. Short overview of my calling:
One sentence

2. Long overview of my calling:
One paragraph

3. A list of fears I will need to overcome:
At least 5

4. A list of possibilities about which I am excited:
At least 5

5. A list of the confidants I've sought advice from:
List friends, families, and spiritual advisors here

6. A summary of the feedback I received from confidants:
A few paragraphs max

7. A list of the professionals I've consulted with:
List coaches, competitors, or collaborators in your industry here

8. A summary of the feedback I received from professionals:
A maximum of a few paragraphs

9. The season I am currently in and what that means to me:
Pick one: discovering, training, or operating

10. Here is the first step I plan to take to live my calling:
2-3 sentences

11.Here is the shape I hope my calling will take in 5 years:
One paragraph

You are welcome to take time to think and pray over this, but no more than 48 hours. Any more means you're probably procrastinating. It's time to start living your calling. Everyone is waiting.

ASK

Am I a natural planner? If yes, what benefits have I seen from it? If no, what consequences have I seen because of it?

_____

_____

_____

_____

_____

_____

_____

_____

_____

_____

_____

BELIEVE

If I fail to plan, I'm planning to fail.

DO   ☐ COMPLETED

Write your two page calling overview, print it, and keep accessible for easy viewing.

"Discipline is doing things we don't necessarily like to achieve the things we love."

JASON BENHAM

DAY 21
Your Life's Work

Happiness expert Gretchen Rubin says there are four stages to enjoying a happy event. (And I'd call discovering your calling a happy event!) The first stage is "anticipation." You've been looking forward to finding your calling for days, weeks, months, and maybe years.

But now that you've found, accepted and committed to your calling, you can begin working through the next ones. Step two is "savoring," which means enjoying the moment. This journey you've embarked on is worth celebrating, so plan something big.

Step three is "expressing," which means sharing the joy

with others. Help your friends, family, and coworkers discover and embark on the journey you've just completed.

Step four is "reflecting," which means looking back on the happy time you've enjoyed. Social media, a natural documentation of our lives, may help you review where you've been. As you embrace your calling, be intentional to take photos and mark important moments along the way.

You haven't just unlocked your calling. You've also unlocked personal fulfillment and happiness. Why? Because not only have you started living the first three steps, but you've started the process all over. Accepting your calling means you have given yourself something to anticipate again.

As you reach for the mountain top—that pinnacle that is your life's work—you're going to continue to grow in accomplishments. This may not happen immediately, but it will happen. Henry Jay Heimlich invented his life-saving maneuver at 54. George Burns received his Oscar at 80. The average age of a Nobel prize winner is 60. So, be patient. You've got a long voyage ahead of you.

And don't forget that the goal isn't the destination, but the journey. You're going to be learning, growing, and expanding along the way as you begin pursuing your life's work.

In just 21 days, you've done the hard work of finding the right road for your life. This is something worth celebrating.

ASK

What has this process revealed to me that I never expected?

_____

_____

_____

_____

_____

_____

_____

_____

_____

_____

BELIEVE

The most fortunate people on earth are those who have found their calling.

DO   ☐ COMPLETED

Go start your new life.

"The goal isn't
the destination,
it's the journey."

UNKNOWN

FINAL STEPS
And Fun Suggestions

As you pursue your true calling, keep a few things in mind. Sometimes we imagine that doing what we're meant to do will feel easy. It's simply not true. Calling is hard work. Really hard work. There will even be seasons of what feels like dead work. You will still have days when you won't feel like going to work and even days when you want to quit. Such is the nature of all work.

But this good work will never be done in vain. It will be work that expands instead of constricts your spirit, leaving you feeling more, not less, alive. It will be work that stretches you, grows you, and helps you reach your potential as a man. It will be work that satisfies not only your hunger, but a hunger in the world. Most of all, it will give you the incomparable feeling that there is a reason and purpose for your existence. It confirms that you are where you are meant to be, doing what you were meant to do.

Before I leave you, I want to offer you a few more resources for your journey.

1. Launch Your Dream
Launch your Dream is the title of the sequel to this book. For those who are built to work for themselves, it's the next natural step in the progression toward the realization of your life's work. While this book was a short self-published book (just under 13,000 words), Launch Your Dream is a traditionally published book with Thomas Nelson. It's 40,000 words designed as a 30-day guide for turning your passion into your profession. In terms of practical advice for chasing a dream, I would call it my own life's greatest work. You can pick up a copy online or anywhere books are sold.

2. StartupCamp.com
For those looking for a more hands-on guide to self-employment, freelancing, or launching your own business, join the over 250,000 monthly readers of my blog and the over 2,000 students enrolled in my 12-month step-by-step program at StartupCamp.com

3. The StartupCamp Podcast
There's a reason we're a top 100 leadership and business podcast on iTunes. Each week I interview bestselling authors, thriving entrepreneurs, and others who are among the most successful people on the planet. Join over 100,000 monthly listeners for a show that will not only strengthen your professional life but will inspire your personal life, too. Simply open up your podcast app on your phone or listen online at StartupCamp. com/Podcast

On social media you can also join over 1 million people who follow my daily posts for creating the business and family you love.

- Facebook.com/DaleJPartridge
- Instagram.com/DalePartridge
- Twitter.com/DalePartridge
- Pinterest.com/DalePartridge

To a life of meaning,

Dale Partridge

END NOTES
For Your Reference

1. John Donne, Devotions Upon Emergent Occasions, (New York: Oxford University Press, 1987), 103-110.

2. Jeanne Meister, "Job Hopping Is the 'New Normal' for Millennials: Three Ways to Prevent a Human Resource Nightmare," Forbes, August 14, 2012, accessed October 9, 2016, http://www.forbes.com/sites/jeannemeister/2012/08/14/job-hopping-is-the-new-normal-for-millennials-three-ways-to-prevent-a-human-resource-nightmare/#1d5ff4b85508.

3. Katharine Brooks Ed.D., "Job, Career, Calling: Key to Happiness and Meaning at Work?," Psychology Today, June 29, 2012, accessed October 12, 2016, https://www.

psychologytoday.com/blog/career-transitions/201206/
job-career-calling-key-happiness-and-meaning-work.

4. Brett and Kate McKay, "Finding Your Calling Part 1,"
The Art of Manliness, May 24, 2010, accessed September
22, 2016, http://www.artofmanliness.com/2010/05/24/
finding-your-calling-part-i-what-is-a-vocation/.

5. Frederick Buechner, Wishful Thinking: A Seeker's
ABC (New York: HarperOne, 1993)

6. Brené Brown, I Thought It Was Just Me (But It Isn't!):
Making the Journey from "What Will People Think?" to
"I Am Enough" (New York: Penguin, 2007).

7. Andy Stanley, Next Generation Leader: 5 Essentials
for Those Who Will Shape the Future (Colorado
Springs: WaterBrook Multnomah, 2003).

8. Laozi, The Sayings of Lao Tzu (London: The Orient
Press, 1904), 35.

TURN YOUR CALLING INTO YOUR CAREER.

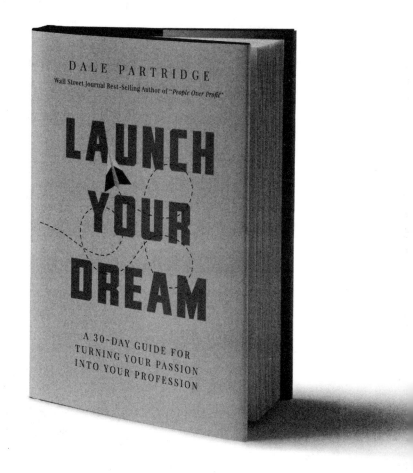

BUILD A BUSINESS THAT CHANGES THE WORLD

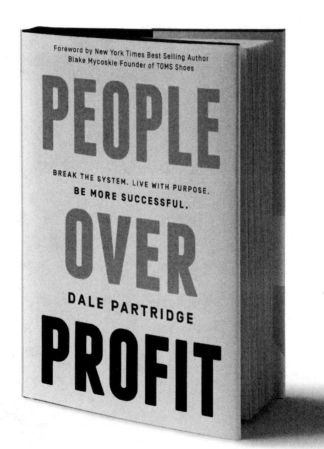

StartupCamp.com/People

DO YOU HAVE A BUSINESS IDEA BUT DON'T KNOW WHERE TO BEGIN?

Enroll in Dale Partridge's 12-month coaching course

- Coching Videos
- PDF Packs
- Study Guides
- Checklists

- Training Articles
- Podcasts
- Video Interviews
- Live Call Q&A's

Create the business and life you love.

StartupCamp.com